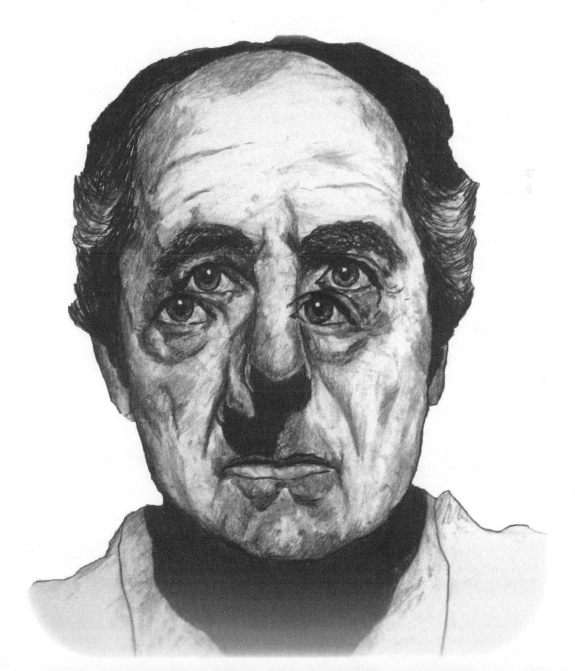

Destruction Myth

poems

Mathias Svalina

CSU Poetry Series
Cleveland State University Poetry Center
Cleveland, Ohio

First edition

13   12   11   10   09   5   4   3   2   1

This book is a title in the CSU Poetry Series,
published by the Cleveland State University Poetry Center,
2121 Euclid Avenue, Cleveland, Ohio 44115-2214
www.csuohio.edu/poetrycenter and is distributed by
SPD /Small Press Distribution, Inc. www.spdbooks.org.

LIBRARY OF CONGRESS CATALOGING-IN-PUBLICATION DATA

Svalina, Mathias.
 Destruction myth : poems / Mathias Svalina. — 1st ed.
   p. cm. — (CSU poetry series)
 ISBN 978-1-880834-87-9 (alk. paper)
 I. Cleveland State University. Poetry Center. II. Title. III. Series.

PS3619.V35D47 2009
811'.6—dc22

                    2009028515

Destruction Myth was designed and typeset in Stone Print, with
Optima display, by Amy Freels.

Cover & additional illustrations: Jake Gillespie, used with permission.

Acknowledgments

Thanks to the editors of these journals who previously published poems from this book: *Absent; The Agriculture Reader; American Letters & Commentary; Bat City Review; Columbia Poetry Review; Copper Nickel; Forklift, Ohio; Handsome; The Hat; Konundrum Engine Literary Review; The Laurel Review; Pleiades; Realpoetik;* & *Tarpaulin Sky.*

A portion of this book appeared as the chapbook *Creation Myths* (New Michigan Press, 2007).

One of these poems appears as part of a video on the *Ninth Letter* website. The video was made by Elisabeth Reinkordt & includes the talents of Patrick Wilkins & Anderson Reinkordt.

This book is indebted to Zachary Schomburg, Heather Green, Ashley Payne & G.C. Waldrep.

Deepest love & thanks to Julia Cohen, the physicist, & to Mary Beth & John Svalina, the chemists.

for Ashley & Alyssa Svalina

Contents

Destruction Myth

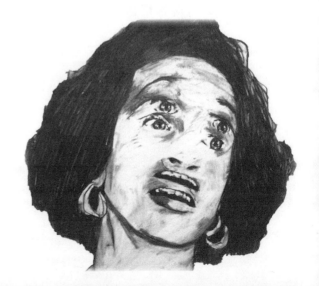

Creation Myth

In the beginning everyone looked like Larry Bird
but everyone did not have the name Larry Bird
& this was confusing. Everyone had a headache
& walked around with furrowed brows. Headaches
hadn't been invented & when people described the pain
they said: *An angry Larry Bird stands on my neck*
& *My head is Larry Bird after missing a layup.*
Even the babies were the size & shape of Larry Bird.
Since everyone looked like Larry Bird they avoided
extravagant events. All the clubs shut down, no one
could watch a Larry Bird dance without understanding
that they danced like this, pursed lips, flagellum legs,
arms like wild fire hoses. The real Larry Bird retired
to his basement. He wore magnifying goggles
& built watches of smaller & smaller dimension.
He built watches so small that he needed a microscope
to affix the springs & levers in the right places.
He built watches so small that he called them cells.
He built watches so small that he called them atoms.

Creation Myth

In the beginning there was a wall.

On one side of the wall there was a city of tall iron buildings & enormous aquariums, the streets clotted & septic with pedestrians. There were three churches: the Church of Money, the Church of Sensual Pleasure & the Church of Hovercrafts.

The land on the other side of the wall was entirely full of hovercrafts, packed in so tightly that any movement required complicated spatial negotiations. The engines of the millions of hovercrafts whirred so loudly that all the hovercraft drivers were deaf.

Once a year the members of the Church of Money would climb over the wall & attempt to steal a hovercraft in order to chop it up & sell its parts for cash. The members of the Church of Hovercrafts would defend the wall to keep the members of the Church of Money on the city-side of the wall.

When a Hovercraftarian would confront a Moneyarian attempting to climb the wall, he or she would first salute his or her opponent. Then he or she would, as the ritual prescribes, offer the Moneyarian some money. The Moneyarian would begin to haggle with the Hovercraftarian. If they reached an acceptable offer the Moneyarian would take the money & donate it to the church. If no offer was found acceptable, the Moneyarian would spit on the Hovercraftarian's shoes.

While all of this was going on the Sensual Pleasurarians would lie in wide waterbeds together, licking each other's navels & inner arms. The Sensual Pleasurarians knew nothing of money, knew nothing of hovercrafts & hovercraft parts. Once they entered the church they ate & drank nothing. They did nothing but lie in the waterbeds & lick each other's skin.

The sound of the hovercrafts could be felt through the earth. The mothers feeding their babies could see it in the rippling surface of the milk. The architects could see it in their shaky pencil lines. The pedestrians could feel it vibrating their knees as they walked the clotted city streets. They called this vibration The Truth. They did their best to ignore it.

Creation Myth

In the beginning there was nothing. But the nothing smelled like bacon. No one could figure out how nothing could: a) have a smell & b) smell like bacon.

Someone suggested that maybe someone who spends a lot of time working the bacon & who hasn't changed out of his work clothes was near. But everyone looked around & confirmed that there was no person who spends a lot of time working the bacon & who hadn't changed out of his work clothes nearby. In fact, there was nothing in existence.

Someone else suggested that perhaps nothingness was a kind of bacon. She put together a chart that showed that it was logically possible that nothingness was a kind of bacon & people listened to her lecture & nodded their heads but secretly they were all thinking about what to eat for dinner. They all wanted to eat some bacon. Some wanted pizza as well.

Someone else suggested that the smell of bacon could be proof of the omnipresence of God. He asked the crowd: *You love bacon, yes?* The crowd grumbled their agreement. *And you love God, yes?* Again they grumbled their agreement. *Is it really so hard to see that God is bacon? That the smell of bacon is the smell of God?*

As it turns out, the people were smelling all that bacon not because nothingness was a kind of bacon or because there was someone who spends a lot of time working the bacon & hadn't changed out of his work clothes nearby but because they were all made of bacon. They'd all been created in God's image. And sometimes the image has a scent.

Creation Myth

In the beginning the children went to children-school & the parents went to parent-school & the killers went to killer-school & the gardeners went to gardener-school. After adjectives they were released. After adverbs they began to slide around the kitchen danglingly & rubber-bandedly. The government grew sloppy, it grew lax & understandingly indulgently caringly considerately.

Soon the people lost their nouns. School became boring-exciting-old-new-salty. Dinner became hot-salty-heavy-tired. Love became sad-gauzy-scaled-sad-necessary-terrifying-dry. People passed into one another's bodies, they collected each other like overburdened coat racks.

Soon they lost their adjectives. School became sittingly-teachingly-yawningly-scraped-kneesedly. Love became twitchingly-twitchingly-twitchingly-twitchingly. When the sun rose one morning all the people had melded into one squirming mass of flesh.

The scientists returned & found this mess of people in the middle of the quaint downtown, blocking the main road of the parade route. The scientists cut little pieces out of the mass of people, freeze-dried them & stored them in the huge warehouse outside town.

Years later the descendents could not understand the failures of their antecedents. The warehouse had become a museum. By then the government had strictly enforced a noun & being-verb only law. People clenched their faces until they looked like catchers' mitts & said: *Block is great-great-great-great-grandfather* & *Block is great-great-*

great-great-grandmother. A woman would look at her husband & say: *Man is husband & Man is man.*

When a child tripped over an electrical cord & fell down to the ground the parents looked first at her broken leg, then at her screaming broken face, then simply walked away.

Creation Myth

He set the first fires as a joke
& the rest were acts of boredom.

He built the first mountains
because there is not much else
to do when you're God.

He built the sky because
he kept bumping his head
on Heaven & cussing.

Omnipotence is lonely.
He's still unclear
as to why he created humans.

He woke up with this great idea
& later in the day
he remembered that he'd had
this great idea, but he couldn't
remember what the idea was.

He tried to remember
but then he thought of humans.
He made them out of clay
& spun them in circles.

He said to the man:
You are master of the woman.
He said to the woman:
You are my most important child.
He said to them both:
You are both divine.

If you think about it
it's a pretty good joke.

Creation Myth

In the beginning there were only streets.
There were streets that led to cliffs,
streets that led to patches of dandelions,
streets that led to other streets,
streets that led to desires & streets that led
to the potential for desires.

Some streets curled into tongue-sized segments.
Some streets were perforated so that the wind whistled dissonant tonalities.
Some streets burrowed into the earth to the molten core.

There was a four-mile stretch of street
in the middle of the Australian outback,
a street floating in the Indian Ocean.

There were streets that were never seen.
There was a street that looked like you
when you were eight years old.
Some streets considered themselves to be houses.
Some streets did not know
they were streets.

There was, however, no Department of Transportation
& over the millennia the streets dissolved into cracks & weeds.
Eventually the living things arrived

& grew bigger & smaller
& there were people & the people
invented cars.

When you're driving a car & you feel the wheel
jerk beneath your hands, it is not the wind
or a pothole. You've driven over the ghost
of an ancient street & your car is crying out
the only way it knows how.

Your car does not love you. Your car knows
what it is to be a car & that cars belong
to the streets. Just as every bird
belongs to the bird feeder. Just as lead
belongs to the pencil. That's how I felt
when I was eight years old
& my home broke apart.

Creation Myth

In the beginning there was a rotting pig corpse. This is gross. I know, I know, I know. I'm sorry to have to tell this story, but I need to explain to all of you why I cannot release your homes from the lost-mail warehouse.

After the blowflies hatched from the rotting pig corpse they flew off in every direction. One blowfly grew angry & became the sun. One blowfly got tired & became the moon. A million blowflies flew out & became the stars. The craftiest blowfly stayed hidden inside the pig's corpse & became the earth. It implanted the corpse with five maggots.

The five maggots hatched as three women & two men. They built a house beside a lake & began to write books that described what it was to be a woman, what is was to be a man.

One maggot-man wrote: *A man is a home with no wings.*
One maggot-man wrote: *A man is a floorboard that never rots.*
One maggot-woman wrote: *A woman is a wooden bucket full of words.*
One maggot-woman wrote: *A woman is a tool used for both digging & killing.*
One maggot-woman wrote: *A woman is a home with potential & a voice.*

The two maggot-men went swimming in the lake & became the written word. One maggot-woman walked out into the woods & became the sound of the voice. Another maggot-woman became the inspiration for art. The last maggot-woman stayed in the house & became the postal service.

Generations later the descendants of the maggot-people found that government demanded that they write letters. Out of protest they refused. They stared at the white faces of envelopes & licked stamp after stamp & stuck them to the walls of their homes.

To break this spirit of rebellion the postal service mailed all of their homes out of town. All the homes ended up in the lost-mail warehouse, the warehouse that had been built atop the last remains of the rotten pig corpse. Everything ends up in the warehouse.

Creation Myth

In the beginning everyone wanted to fight to the death. This made shopping difficult & also lovemaking & most everything else. Pools of blood slimed the streets & people paired off in clumsy dances of elbows, bites & gouges.

Panting & exhausted, the remaining humans called a truce. One human said: *We need to find a different outlet for our aggressions*. The crowd agreed. Another human said: *We can split up into teams & try to kill the other teams*. The crowd agreed.

The humans split up into four teams & spent all their time killing the other teams. Eventually one team had killed all the other teams & they sat in their locker room, icing down their raw knuckles, eyeing each other.

One teammember said: *Now we need to find a new outlet for our aggressions*. The team agreed. Another teammember said: *We can build a ladder that reaches the moon*. The team agreed.

The team gathered wood & tools & stacked them in the tallest teammember's spacious backyard. They spent seven days & seven nights working on the ladder, eating cold fried chicken & drinking Mr. Pibb.

On the eighth day the ladder was done & they rested it up against the moon. The tallest teammember said: *This is my backyard, so I will climb to the moon first*. The team did not agree. The quickest teammember said: *I am the quickest so I should go first*. The team did not agree. The smallest teammember said: *I am the smallest so I should go first*.

The smallest teammember threw some cold fried chicken at the quickest teammember & hit him right in the ear hole, so the quickest teammember killed the smallest teammember. And then one killed another & so on & so on. Soon the backyard was covered in blood & only the strongest teammember remained alive.

The strongest teammember climbed the ladder to the moon. It took him seven days & seven nights & when he arrived on the moon he was tired, hungry & thirsty. The moon was delightful. The strongest teammember biked some nice bike paths, stopped for pizza at a great little place near the river, had a few locally brewed beers & stayed at an inexpensive yet clean hotel.

When it came time for the strongest teammember to return to the earth he found himself sad. He said to himself: *I don't want to leave the moon. No one wants to fight to the death here. There are no teams & aggressions. Everything smells like soap.*

Creation Myth

In the beginning everything I said exploded. I would say: *I am holding a glass of ice water* & the glass of ice water would explode. I would mumble to myself: *Where's my cell phone* & hear a small boom in the bedroom. My first word was daddy. After that I didn't speak for ten years.

I tried to use my explosions for good. I said shuffling feet & never heard that scrape again. I said crooked politicians but the next day there was a new batch of them giving press conferences after the memorial services. I almost said nuclear warheads & then decided that this might be unwise.

I made lists of words I could not say. Words like oak, mother & pills. Words like journalists, femurs & workers. I would walk around with my buddies after the bars closed & once I forgot & said: *That Dan Rather is a respectable news source, huh?* & everyone froze & Sutter punched me in the shoulder. It took two weeks until there were new newspapers & they were all a little thin. I told my fiancée I loved her & just like that the love was gone.

In the spaces where the things used to be, in the craters left after the explosions, a new kind of mold grows. It grows orange on some days & yellow on others. It grows quickly & always toward me. I'm not sure what will happen when the mold reaches me but I hope I will be brave. I hope I will not say mold. There is so much I shouldn't tell you. I know your name is Seashore. But your name is Animal. That's my name too.

Creation Myth

My mother & father are both chemists. They light their ranch-style home with Bunsen burners & drink from glass beakers. They created the universe in 1968 when they dripped one foul-smelling chemical into a clear chemical that smelled like ice & formed my brother. The universe was a small apartment in South Side Chicago. My Aunt & Uncle lived downstairs inside a camera lens.

Each morning my mother & father would drip chemicals from an eyedropper into a frying pan & the chemicals became French toast. When I was five they created a city that they called New Orleans. They created fire ants & water moccasins. When I was ten they created a new kind of bone that breaks.

My mother & father, the chemists, stayed up late every night mixing chemicals into new creations, their goggles steaming up with concentration. They created tall neighbors with cigarettes & dry hands. They created aboveground pools with blue plastic sides. Toilets full of urine. Collies. New hats. Things I could never have imagined appeared every morning like tents.

When I clip my nails I watch the clippings dissolve immediately into chemicals. Likewise with cut hair. When I die I will prove my mother & father correct. The chemicals into which my body will wilt will be stored on a wooden shelf in brown bottles with rubber stoppers. I had a perfect moment of clarity in the back of Mike Bunn's car while Pittsburgh unfolded into a paper swan. Even this I know they created with chemicals.

There was a shining new bike. There was a dog that jumped into my bed. There was a red bottle. A set of nun-chucks. A yellow dress. Every new thing made me cry tears of bromine, which immediately evaporated. It was a laboratory. I was a child.

Creation Myth

God created the world over the span of four years.
He would get all excited about it & work really hard for a few days
& then he would watch some movies & get out of the mood
of staying up late crafting mountains & deciding where to put all the Shell stations.
He would hang out, popping pills & listening to the coda from "Layla" over & over
again.

But then he would be cooking eggs or cleaning the toilet & think: *Fuck! The world!*
And for a couple of days he would work really hard again,
it was during these active periods that he created New Zealand & piano concertos.

After four years God was updating his Facebook page & wrote:
It may not be good enough, it may not be the best world ever, but its my world & I'm just
sick of tinkering with it, so I'm going to give it a name & call it done & move on to
something else.
He did this. He called his world Des Moines & got in bed to take a nap but he
accidentally set the alarm for AM instead of PM
& he never woke up again & this is why there is only one world
& why it is called Des Moines.

Des Moines consists of single-family homes & several different retirement
    residences.
Des Moines consists of eight hospitals.
Des Moines consists of new construction, replacing previously rural farm fields.
Des Moines feels like warm lake water.
Des Moines has some nice shopping; it is the nexus of God's will.

All things in Des Moines are made up of the five elements:
1. badly bleached hair
2. shoeboxes full of old mix tapes
3. mistakes
4. water
5. dirt

Creation Myth

In the beginning the registrar
took a left hook to the jaw.

He filed a complaint
with the department of left hooks.

He waited for weeks
but there was no reply.

He sharpened a spoon
into a shiv

& stabbed the guy
who'd given him the left hook.

Blood unspooled
over the whole earth.

This blood
is what you call the ocean.

You like to swim
in blood.

Creation Myth

The world began with the beat of a drum.
The drummer was in a metal band
so he was drumming really fast
& things started changing rapidly.

The metal singer sang: *Deeply satanic*
vapors drift inside your blood
& a man named Deeply Satanic arose.
The town needed a mayor,
so he became Mayor Deeply Satanic.

The metal singer sang: *Bloody bile*
drips through the priest's fingers
& a man named Bloody Bile arose.
He liked to kayak on the rapids
so he became a kayaking instructor.

The metal guitarist shredded a solo
& the solo came to life as a woman.
Solo had a knack for engines
so she became the town mechanic.

By the time the metal band
had finished their metal song
the town was fully populated

with florists, teachers, pre-school teachers,
bankers, plumbers & baristas.

Each house held five people.
It was always three against two.
The children against the parents,
the women against the men.
They argued about politics over dinner.
On Sundays they went out to the batting cages
& saw an action film at the theater.

Creation Myth

Two roommates were making soup & noticed that they'd forgotten some of the ingredients. The grocery store was only a few blocks away so they figured that they could leave the stove on low & be back in ten minutes. Unfortunately they were gone forever & over time the soup grew systemic order.

There was the initial hierarchy of the solid. The slices of carrots laughed at the chunks of celery that were almost liquid. The yellow chunks of potato mocked the broth. The hard lentils at the bottom of the pan stayed quiet, but smugly so.

As the cooking continued the starches broke down. The carrots began to dissolve. The potatoes slipped from their skins. A new ideology arose, one of regionalism. There were areas of the soup that were still defined by the qualities of carrot one could find in them; the lentil sludge still held the bottom of the pan; there were still spots where the potatoes could feel like it was important to be a potato.

Eventually the soup became a uniform sludge of matter. Without anybody to hate or be hated the soup mostly spent its time convecting around the pot, watching the passing particles of soup. A new game arose called "What Kind of Vegetable Were You?" In this game the passing particles of soup would guess what the others were & if they guessed correctly they would win.

The problem was that no particle could remember what they had once been. Soon they could not even remember what the names of the vegetables were & the passing particles would say things like: *You were once a piece of adorning* or *You were obviously a slice of quoin.* Because of the way the game worked the particle would always respond: *Why yes, I was. You are very astute.*

Before one particle could respond to another, the convections of the soup would have pushed them apart. But it did not matter to whom one addressed one's guess or responses. Despite the fact that the information was incorrect the particles of soup were always flattered to be identified.

Creation Myth

In the beginning there was a woman with a toolbox full of paperclips. She walked around the void paperclipping water to earth, paperclipping fish to the lakes, paperclipping tears to the fish's eyes, paperclipping salt to the tears.

Eventually she ran out of paperclips & she sat back & watched the paperclipped world interact. Each time a wave hit the beach a paperclip popped off & she had to rush over & repaperclip the ocean to the shore. Each time a person kissed another person the paperclips that affixed their identities popped off & she had to rush over & repaperclip the correct identity to the correct person. Sometimes she mixed them up.

Panting for breath, she sat below a pear tree onto which she had paperclipped a thousand white petals. The wind blew & the paperclips popped off & the petals drifted from the pear tree.

This won't do, she said to herself. *Everything is so mutable.* So she bought a vat of superglue & superglued the ocean to the shore & superglued rawhide chewbones to dogs' mouths & superglued the leaves to the azalea bushes & superglued sadness to the people who were crying & superglued happiness to the people who laughing.

For a few weeks she took a vacation. She went to the beach, drank a bunch of cheap beer on the sand & had a lot of sex with a backpacker from Denmark to whom she had superglued the smell of honeysuckle.

When she returned from her vacation she was expecting her inbox & her voicemail to be full, but they were empty. She looked out her window & saw that everything was still. She noticed that people who had been crying were now dead from sadness, the leaves had rotted on the azalea bushes, the people who had been happy had split their faces open from too much smiling & were lying in pools of their own blood, laughing like champagne.

This won't do, she said to herself. *Everything is too fixed*. So she bought a humungous papershredder & shredded the oceans & shredded the mountains & shredded the people & shredded their pets & shredded the wind & shredded the grogginess of morning & shredded the grogginess of drunkenness & shredded the joy of watching one's brother get married & shredded the joy of watching one's abusive boyfriend get his knuckles shattered with a ball peen hammer.

Once every thing in the world had been shredded the woman threw it all into a big blue plastic vat, threw a family of raccoons into the vat, closed the vat's lid & went back to the beach. The raccoons will take care of things, she said to herself. She walked along the beach, hoping to find another backpacker, but she had shredded them all. She drank cheap beer alone on the sand. She watched the sun set every night.

She kept a little notebook in her pocket. She had written the words "Random Thoughts" on the cover in whiteout. Every day she opened it & tapped her pen against her teeth & sipped her beer & tried to think of something random.

Creation Myth

A little boy cut a circle
out of yellow paper
& this became the sun.

The little boy laid
a sheet of blue paper
on the floor & this
became the oceans.

The little boy cut
a daisy chain of people
out of paper & hung
it on the wall & this
became humanity.

It was nice for a while.
The people were happy
to just exist, they liked
the sun & the oceans,
they liked talking to people,
they liked how the wall felt
against their backs.

Eventually they tired
of hanging on the wall.
They wanted these things:
to swim in the oceans,
to tan on their backs,
to talk to more than two people.

They passed their plan
along the chain of people.
On the count of three
they would all pull their
arms & legs in, ripping
them all from one another.

On three they all pulled.
It was the first ripping sound
the world ever knew,
this world used to cutting.

It worked. The people
fell from the wall. Some
fell in the oceans, waterlogged
& sank to the bottom. Some
drifted near the sun
& burned up. Most fell
on the earth but realized
that they were paper
& incapable of mobility.

They stayed in the spot
where they'd fallen. Those
lucky enough to have fallen
near other people talked constantly.

All they talked about
was how they missed the wall.

Creation Myth

Human life begins
at the moment
of contraception.

Prior to that
there is the frog stage,
the fern stage
& the stage of melee.

Theorists have proposed
another ten dimensions of life
but experimental science
has yet to prove them.

Nothing without thumbs
is human.

Creation Myth

Before there were people
there were ghosts.
They walked around
holding radios & eyedroppers,
looking quizzically at each other,
trying to understand
what the street signs said.

Something was ringing
& it wouldn't stop.
The ghosts gathered
around the ringing,
shuffling back & forth
on feathery feet,
ghost-heads lolling
on shadowy necks.

There was a voice
& all the ghosts started:
No one can feed the baby.
No one can feed the baby.

Creation Myth

There was a bunny with a broken leg
& a mink with an empty stomach.

Somehow they coexisted peacefully
& were able to create the world.

When Hollywood heard about this
they sent a team of idea people out to meet them.

The idea people were so crass
that the bunny & the mink uncreated the world.

They drank up all the oceans
& hairdried all the clouds.

They knocked down all the mountains
& flicked the switch that turned the sun off.

They sat together in the darkness,
neither one really knowing what to say.

The mink leaned over to the bunny,
put his paw on his friend's shoulder,

said: *Well it's been a wild ride*
& bit the bunny's throat out.

Creation Myth

In the beginning I was a little thing in the center of a star. I had a lot of work to do & I liked to check things off of my to-do list. Then my parents appeared & made me & then my voice appeared & I had words to say.

Soon I was walking into & out of buildings constantly. The sky hazed over with streetlight: the stars might as well have disappeared. The stars fell to the ground & I picked them up & ate them like caramel. This continued & I forgot where I'd forgotten the hands & the feet.

When I died the star welcomed me back to its center & asked me what I'd learned. I told the star about all the people I'd met & forgotten & all the things I'd printed out on printers. I told the star about all the beautiful shelves they have on Earth.

Then my parents knocked on the star again & they made me & they asked me to come down for dinner. Beneath the table I saw my to-do list, which I must have lost years ago. I crawled under the table to pick up my to-do list & when I did I was completely alone.

Creation Myth

A man was preparing a lasagna but then he realized that this lasagna was a lot of food & he didn't have anyone to share it with so he decided that he would make some people first. He put the lasagna in the fridge & went out to the hardware store. He bought a paper bag full of nails & he bought a couple tubes of caulk.

The people he made with caulk & nails were very rude. He'd expected them to be somewhat gracious to him, considering that he'd brought them into existence, but instead they ripped his couch & loveseat & left globs of caulk all over his carpet. Because they were so rude he didn't bother to cook the lasagna. Instead he threw the caulk & nail people into a metal barrel & set them on fire.

He went out to the craft store & bought some yarn & glitter & made people out of this. These people were a little too nice, they followed him around the house wrapping their yarny arms around him in warm, yearning hugs. Within an hour he was covered in glitter. When he rubbed his eyes he got glitter in them & this was too much. He grabbed all the yarn & glitter people & tossed them into the metal barrel & set them on fire.

He went out to the rendering plant & bought a vat of lard & made people out of lard. These people were OK but he couldn't stand the smell & they went into the burn-barrel. Following them he had to burn the people made of handmade paper, the people made of elm leaves, the people made of starling feathers & even the people made of eggs benedict.

After all this making & burning of people he decided that he'd had enough he would just eat his lasagna alone, but he was tired so he took a nap. When he woke up he walked into the kitchen & saw a huge line of black stuff leading from the door to the kitchen.

He opened the refrigerator door & saw hundreds of people made of ash inside. They had eaten the lasagna, but they were still hungry. The people made of ash jumped out of the fridge & knocked the man onto the linoleum floor & began to eat him. The mixture of blood & ash turned their bodies into flesh. They went out & looked for apartments to rent. It was summer, so there were a lot of good deals. Most of them got their first month's rent for free.

Creation Myth

In the beginning I was a thesaurus.

In the beginning I was five years old, walking through a fire ant hill in Louisiana. My first memory was the pain of their bites. How my father picked me up & washed the ants off my legs & my screaming.

In the beginning I was a tree limb in the back yard. When I mowed the lawn I piled the clippings between three trees, a magic space of decomposing hair.

In the beginning I watched my child-face in the mirror & saw the beautiful skull beneath those cupcake cheeks.

In the beginning the girl across the street took me out into the humid swelter of the cement gutters & said *close your eyes*.

In the beginning I wrecked my dad's Volvo into a tree, driving out of a park at 2AM with the cops chasing after us.

In the beginning I could not stop reading all night. How hot the covers. How cold the night air through the screened in windows.

In the beginning I opened the door & saw my older brother crying in the dark of his bedroom. I closed the door. No one spoke in my house ever again.

In the beginning I met a girl with red hair & never thought we would one day be in love. And that we would one day not be in love.

In the beginning my mother & father met at the Water Works.

In the beginning my grandfather took my grandmother dancing & that night knew that they would be married.

In the beginning there was a mountain.

In the beginning there was an ocean.

In the beginning there were twelve kids in the basement of Ellen Caskie's house reading the wallpaper to the fry cooks.

In the beginning a man screamed into the mike & the floor was a mass of living papers.

In the beginning my stomach hummed with streetlights.

Years later my older brother told me that it was not my father who'd picked me up, but him.

Creation Myth

In the beginning there were a bunch of evildoers & criminals & villains. They walked around looking sneaky & hid in the shadows. Eventually they grew bored of having no one to victimize so they created a race of smiles. The smiles could only look in the direction of the sun. They drank sugary drinks & read *Reader's Digest* Condensed Novels.

The evildoers, criminals & villains followed the smiles around & pulled wallets from their pockets, pulled car keys out of their hands & sold them worthless property. The smiles, however, only smiled in response to their victimization.

One criminal fell in love with a smile. They rented a hotel room & had dirty, dirty sex for three days. Both of them grew pregnant & nine months later the criminal gave birth to Civilization & the smile gave birth to Religion. Civilization & Religion got married when they were sixteen. They had a large family. Every Sunday they would have family dinner, kids running around the house, dogs barking, tomato sauce burnt in the cast iron pot.

The criminal squeezed the smile's hand, looking out over the kids & grandkids & great-grandkids. The two looked each other in the eye, lovingly. The criminal said: *We have created the world.* The two held hands. *Yes,* the smile said. *They're all going to die.*

Creation Myth

In the beginning there was a sk8r girl & a sk8r boy & they were deciding what kind of world to create. The sk8r boy wanted a world that was entirely downhill so he could skate really fast. The sk8r girl wanted a world that was flat so she could practice all her rad moves. They split the world in two. The sk8r girl tore up the flat part of the world with her rad moves. The sk8r boy skated faster than anyone had or ever will.

Soon, however, the sk8r girl realized that rad moves were nothing without someone to show the rad moves to. The sk8r boy realized that he was going so fast he would never be able to stop.

The sk8r girl sat on her skateboard & looked down at her shoes. *These could use a cleaning,* she said to herself & she went off to find a spigot. The sk8r boy sat down on his skateboard, which was moving exponentially faster in the perpetually downhill world. *I miss sk8r girl,* he said to himself. *This is as boring as I imagined the flat world would be.*

Sk8r girl returned to her board with freshly scrubbed shoes. Lying with her back on the board, looking up at the clouds, rocking herself slowly forward & back, she thought: *I used to think sk8r boy was so cool. Now I think he's a dweeb.*

Creation Myth

In the beginning there was a big puddle of honey & millions of ants surrounded the puddle & after the ants came the mice whose faces grew sticky with honey, honey dripping from their long whiskers & after the mice came the dogs who lapped at the honey until their fur was matted & coated with honey & after the dogs came the bears who spooned up big globs of honey with their stony paws & after the bears came the humans but by then all the honey had been eaten.

The humans stood in the spot where the honey puddle had been & looked at each other & cried. One of them invented speaking & they all complained about how much they were looking forward to the honey & one of them invented the plough & they built a farm on the spot where the honey puddle had been & one of them invented guns & they went out into the world & shot all the mice, dogs & bears.

The ants watched all of this from their anthill. They patted their swollen bellies. They laughed at the humans & their complicated objects. They passed bowls of honey around the crowd & drank deep of the honey & passed out from too much honey. So they did not see the humans inventing a new kind of ant that feeds on honey-eating ants.

Once the ant-eating ants ate all the honey-eating ants they turned on the humans & ate all the humans. Once the ant-eating ants ate all the humans they turned on each other & ate each other. Eventually there was only one ant-eating ant alive, the only creature alive in the world. He returned to the spot where the honey puddle had been, sat down & watched the sunset over the foothills & then ate his own thorax.

Creation Myth

In the beginning there was a map of the East Coast that didn't have any of the highways on it. The doctors came & checked it out. The diagnosis was melancholy so they hooked the map up to an IV & pumped it full of Demerol.

One of the nurses noticed that the map was printed with a strange ink so she had it sent down to the lab. The lab technicians ascertained that the ink was dyed milk, which made the detectives suspect that the map was involved in the crime.

Three detectives approached the map & accused it of being in on the crime. When it wouldn't talk the doctors pumped it full of sodium pentothal. Delegates from the UN watched all of this through a peephole.

The delegates returned to the UN to tell them that the secret was out; the map had been discovered. They rented some Chris Farley movies & ordered pizzas & had a brainstorming session about what to do.

The UN guy from Russia suggested that they build an infinite number of nesting dolls. One for every potential person there could be on earth. Because there were no better ideas & they were out of pizza the other UN delegates agreed to this & they allocated some money & started construction.

The first nesting doll was infinitely big, the subsequent dolls incrementally smaller. After they had constructed an infinite number of dolls they folded the map up until it was the size of an electron & placed it inside the smallest nesting doll.

They built a rocket to shoot the dolls out into space but when they fired it they realized their error. The biggest doll was infinitely big so it had nowhere to go. Trying to make the best of the situation they created a new religion based on the dolls.

The central tenet of this religion is that there is a tiny map inside of each of us but only when every person is nested inside of each other will anyone be able to read where the highways are on the map. The eternal search is for the people who are one increment bigger & one increment smaller than you.

People walked around wielding slide rules, calculating logarithms, establishing the correct hierarchy of nesting. When someone found one that they were supposed to be next to they followed them around. Soon there were long chains of people that followed each other around. They tattooed maps on their foreheads, they bought increasingly flashy slide rules of ivory & mahogany.

The only ones who didn't believe the religion were the truckers. They rode the highways every day. The highways were filled with ghosts of maps that fluttered by night in the wakes. The ghosts howled at the passing trucks. *New legends,* they howled. *We need new legends.*

Creation Myth

In the beginning there was a pen that drew itself into existence & then drew all the grasses & flowers & then drew all the trees & mountains & then drew all the rivers & lakes & then drew all the firemen & cops & then drew all the militaries & intelligence agencies & then drew all the traitors & murderers & then drew all the victims & the barbed wire.

The pen was tired & running low on ink. It knew it could only draw one more thing before running completely dry. It made a list of things it could draw: art, breakfast, books about insects, bags of oranges, fancy handmade glass paperweights. But at this point in its list the ink ran out.

Without any ink to move itself the pen was stuck & had to watch as the militaries outlined in its own confident black lines fought against each other, as the traitors with their expertly shaded dark eyes threw their outlines of hand grenades at each other, as the murderers spilled blood on the outlines of flowers, the blood shaded in with thick, black crosshatched lines.

If I had it all to do over again, the pen thought, *I would have first drawn another pen & then drawn jars of colorful ink. It's not so bad to see blood spilled over the world I've drawn but it blacks out all my lines.* And the pen was correct. This is the first rule of aesthetics: when they are soaked in blood there is no difference between one tree & another, between a traitor & a soldier.

Creation Myth

In the beginning there was a book
but every time a villager read the book
it meant something different to her
than it did to her friend or her mother.

The villagers fought over the correct interpretation.
Mothers ripped earrings from their sons' ears.
Children stuffed their parents' mouths with gauze.
Priests bludgeoned bakers. Twins disagreed.

Eventually someone decided to throw the book
down the well, but when she picked it up
a shower of keys fell from its pages,
each key labeled for a particular villager.

There were no locks at that time
so the villagers took their keys home
to their basements & garages & built locks
& locked up everything they owned.

They locked up their houses & bikes first.
Then they locked up their drawers & their pockets.
One villager built a lock for his mouth
& then another built a lock for his eyes.

Years later a team of scientists in white coats
discovered the village. All the villagers
had locked themselves completely still
& only a few sneezes revealed that they were alive.

The scientists radioed in for a team of pickpockets
who stole the keys from the locked villagers.
But even the pickpockets could not be of help
because none of the keys opened any of the locks.

Creation Myth

In the beginning there was a gun.
Before that the world
was only gunpowder & steel.

The gun was an infant,
until it turned twenty-one
& then he shot a priest.

The gun had a lot of personal issues
& wrote some sad poems
through the skulls of depressed teenagers.

The gun was walking in the park
thinking about sad things
when he met a baby monkey.

The baby monkey got the gun's phone number.
The gun waited by the phone
but the monkey never called.

Creation Myth

Creation is an ugly word, with its white canvases & flabby slabs of bacon. It has the sound of a purgative disease, pinky-thick worms in the dissected pig's intestines, a tattered stuffed badger with fluff spilling from its empty eyehole. The word creation wants to dissolve while you say it. It wants you to dissolve while you say it.

Here are a few beautiful words:
Comatose,
Textual, &
Sledgehammer.

Other ugly words include:
Bankruptcy,
Diffident,
KFC,
Pug,
Truth,
Sensitive,
Ranch, &
Catherine.

Creation Myth

In the beginning there was the void. There was a tuba. The tuba wanted to play some polka. There was a fox. The fox wanted to eat a vole. Somebody dropped a bunch of paperclips. The paperclips were fine being a tangled mass of paperclips hanging in the void. Paperclips don't complain.

The fox attempted to blow the tuba, hoping that this sound would create some voles or at least a couple of trash cans full of old tuna salad but the tuba's mouthpiece was shaped for humans & all the fox did was bruise his sensitive nose.

The fox unbent all the paperclips to form them into the skeleton of a vole, thinking it would then come to life & he could eat it. He made a pretty good likeness of a vole skeleton, considering that all he had was paperclips & no opposable thumbs.

The paperclip vole skeleton-like object did not come to life. It hung in the void just like the tuba & the fox.

The tuba tried to imagine some polka songs, thinking that this might create something but he could only remember the tuba parts.

The paperclips felt content, which means (for a paperclip) very tiny.

The fox sat inside the bell of the tuba with his nose on his paws. He didn't look out into the void because there is no void to look out into. A void is a void, nothing to get all maudlin about.

In order to insult the three, the void named them Pierre, Henri & Antoine but they did not get the joke (or if the paperclip-vole-skeleton did it did not care). The void was disappointed with its creations. It created a soft-serve ice cream machine & climbed inside & thereafter it was known as the world.

The void said to the soft-serve ice cream machine: *Knock, knock.*
Soft-serve ice cream machine: *Who's there?*
The void: *Tuba.*
Soft-serve ice cream machine: *Tuba who?*
The void: *Tuba toothpaste.*
Soft-serve ice cream machine:
The void:
Soft-serve ice cream machine: *What's toothpaste?*
The void: *Oh, just something I was thinking about creating.*

Creation Myth

After the beginning of everything the suicide rate increased drastically. This became a hot news item & scientists wearing tooth-white coats & monocles appeared on the evening television to discuss the causes of this increase. Some blamed the degradation of the family. Some blamed the lack of truly good sandwich shops in Lincoln, Nebraska. Others stared silently at the camera & allowed their stern faces to signify their interpretations of the data.

After the politicians & the frameworkers union & the monocled scientists of NASA got involved there was some quick action. One of the frameworkers had recently checked out that Martin Amis book *Time's Arrow* from the library & he convinced the politicians & the monocled scientists that the only way to combat this increase in the suicide rate would be to return to a time before creation.

A call went out to all the listservs & blogs, it was stamped across the monocled news-reporters' shiny heads & ran along the bottom of the television screens below their heads. It said: *Help Fight Suicide; Reverse Creation; Hefty Reward.*

There were the inevitable swimming pool accidents & lawsuits but finally a group of young-buck newly-monocled scientists from a rural college at the bottom of a steep hill produced a machine that would turn back time.

The monocled administrators in NASA appropriated the technology, which, incidentally, fits in the back pocket of your jeans. They pressed the white button to engage the machine & immediately everything began to run backwards. Bullets returning to guns, babies plopping into their mothers' bellies & slowly disappearing. The newspapers reported that the monocled scientists were pleased with the results.

Creation Myth

In the beginning there were only borders, because no one had created the spaces within the borders. The borders all had fancy dance moves with names like The Snake's Lower Intestine Is Not A Game, The Carpal Tunnel Twister, & True Love.

Because borders grow bored without people, they created three women. The borders gave each of the three women their own iPod filled with the same music. The women, however, set the iPods to Shuffle & thereafter they could never agree on a unified version of reality.

One woman started a surprisingly clean theme park outside a tarpit.
One woman shaved her fingerprints off & became a tangle of hair.
One woman curled up on the couch with a pint of ice cream & her softest fleece
    blanket & fell asleep watching silent films.

Silent-Film's armies attacked Tarpit's theme park & soaked the soil with the blood of the defeated. The armies found that they liked the theme park & rebuilt it out of marble & gold. They called the marble parts Earth & the gold parts Sky & the tarpit Our Homeland. No one would ever again return to Our Homeland.

The third woman with the shaved fingerprints is still waiting to make her move. They call her The Ocean. They call her The Disturbing Sublimity of Eternity. She lives in a nice split-level apartment in the heart of the revitalized historic district of downtown Norman, Oklahoma.

She looks like the flatness of thought revealed to be wool.

She looks like this: HUH.

Creation Myth

In the beginning there was a hole in the basement floor. Below the hole there was a computer that had learned how to speak. Unfortunately the computer had not learned the virtues of comfortable, amicable silence between companions. All day long the computer spoke to the hole. Mostly it told the hole about what it was up to, narrating in real time.

Now I am running an application called Probutter, which gives me the semblance of the flavor of real butter.

Now I'm running an application called RealTears that makes me have the feeling of crying.

Now I am running an application called Automator that allows me to continue talking without having anything to say.

Creation Myth

In the beginning the only job was unwrapping the mummy. It takes a long time to unwrap a mummy. Sometimes the mummy moves or sneezes & you have to wrap it back up again & restart the process from the beginning. Sometimes the mummy cries & everyone has to leave the room & stand outside eating wedges of oranges & drinking juice boxes. Sometimes the mummy cries forever.

Eventually the people were almost done unwrapping the mummy so they decided to have a parade to celebrate its final unwrapping. They paraded their long-range missiles, tanks & other heavy artillery through the streets of the downtown, tearing up the asphalt. People lined the streets, waving the flags of as-of-yet unnamed nations. Some of them had a sense of humor; they waved flags with pictures of the mummy on it. Some of them had a sense of tragedy; they waved flags stained with tears.

After the parade came the ritual of the fireworks & the ritual of the babies. Then the almost-unwrapped mummy was raised high off the street. The band played the appropriate music. The people leaned forward, aiming their digital cameras over the heads of the crowd. The people unwrapped the final wrappings that held the mummy. Inside the wrappings there was a hive of wasps. Each wasp wore a nametag sticker reading: *Hello, My Name is Citizen.*

Creation Myth

In the beginning there was a lot of walking up the down-escalators & finding flecks of gold dust in the garden. Then there was something called the Big Bang, which everyone heard about on the radio the next morning. After that people would greet strangers in the street by saying *G3* or *F7* or *A13*. They would awaken in the middle of the night & shake their spouse or partner until they woke up & ask: *Who is that guy on the motorcycle?*

I used to be the guy who had to fix the escalators. I used to be the one to plant the gold flecks in the gardens. I had a van that I drove all over town. I had a to-do list that was four pages long. After the big bang no one wanted me to plant new cherry trees. People spackled their own holes. When I would see old friends they would shake my hand & ask: *How are you doing?*

People stopped caring. They balanced their checkbooks. They kissed each other good night after brushing their teeth. They wore helmets when they rode their bikes. They used bookmarks. They sold their snakes on eBay. They gave their blood away in Ziploc bags.

I don't know who the guy is. The guy on the motorcycle. But he's coming. I don't know why I know this but I know this. He's coming & he's going to save us.

Creation Myth

In the beginning
there was a book
by Italo Calvino.

The book had hind legs
growing where its
arms should've been.

The book ripped
its own pages out
& died. This sacrifice

inspires all great
books. They want
to be empty covers.

They eye your
whole pages & fancy
you confetti.

This is why we
bow low before
entering a cave.

Creation Myth

In the beginning there was a bowl of hair dye mixed with cologne. This produced three cops. The cops each had two guns. They stood in a triangle & pointed their guns at one another. They had been trained not to fire until fired upon & they waited. It was humid. They grew sweaty with tension.

Somewhere close by, a chickadee leaned toward another chickadee & asked: *Have you heard the one about the Jewish guy who joins the Church of Latter Day Saints?* The other chickadee responded: *I've never even heard of Judaism before.* Both chickadees laughed.

Because this was the first laughter in the world it alarmed the three cops pointing their guns at each other & they began shooting. Each of their bullets crashed into each other in midair & fell to the earth. Where they fell, buildings began to grow.

The bullets grew into castles & prisons & temples & state capitols. The bullet fragments grew into suits & power ties & these suits & power ties began to grow people to fit inside themselves. Soon there were enough people grown that the legislature voted in favor of a tax decrease. They held books over their heads like cutlasses.

The cops continued firing. They shot at one another for so long that they forgot why they were shooting. They forgot whom they were shooting. Eventually they forgot who they were. They forgot what shooting was. If you asked one of them their name they would respond: *Cologne. Hair dye cologne.*

Creation Myth

In the beginning there was nothing but unicorns. There were so many unicorns that a splinter group of unicorns grew tired of being so special & cut off their horns & sold their horns on eBay. One collector in Turkey bought all the cut unicorn horns & hung them on the walls of his castle along with some saints' relics & ancient Coptic erotica.

The collector's son would often walk around the castle alone, his father & mother off attending one gaudy soirée or another. He would stare at the Coptic erotica & know that the cold empty castle was somehow his body & that these relics & erotic paintings & unicorn horns were the only things inside the drafty abyss of his body. The boy never left the castle. Every night he ate dinner alone.

Years later the boy had grown into a man & he inherited his father's castle & all of his prized collectibles. For the first time the boy exited the castle. The world outside the castle was only a great white blankness. There were no unicorns or Coptic-speaking people having contorted sex or even soirees in Monaco. There was only a great white blankness extending infinitely in every direction.

The man realized that he was right. The castle was the only thing that truly existed. He poured a gallon of gasoline on his father's rhino-hide couch & tossed a lit match. He walked back out of the castle & saw that the white blankness was gone. Instead dead olive trees in parallel rows extended out into infinity.

When the historians wrote of these events they organized them under the category of "Genesis." The cover of the state-approved textbook on Genesis is a photograph of a unicorn with its mane flapping wildly in a storm-wind. Behind it the world is burning to death.

Creation Myth

In the beginning there was a great flood that destroyed the cities & then someone started a small fire that set off all the smoke alarms. Everyone died except for the fox, the word & the blender. The blender said to the fox & the word: *We shall start a new civilization that will not replicate the prejudices & iniquities of the former civilization.*

Pretty soon the blender & the fox realized that the word was kind of a jerk. He wore mismatching Converse All-Stars, he had a big collection of collectable fantasy knives & he liked to talk about his knives all the time. They buried him up to his neck in drying cement so that he could continue to talk but would not be able to purchase any more collectible fantasy knives.

Another person I hate is this guy Richard I went to elementary school with. He was super smart & I was sort of a loser & we became friends because no one else would talk to us. I really screwed him over. I hear he's teaching at Caltech now. Haven't thought about him in years.

Creation Myth

In the beginning the birds grew wings out of their chests. This caused them to fly in such a way that their heads dangled painfully. The birds had a meeting out beyond the woodshed & wrote a communiqué to the bird-makers. Each bird signed it in his or her own bird blood.

This is what the communiqué said: *Wings were meant for flying with heads turned upwards. We do not want the babies to see us this way. We do not want the babies to cry. They used to have their eggs. Now they only have us. And we need you to put our wings onto backs.*

The bird-makers received the communiqué with the mail but they were not in the habit of checking the mail, figuring that anything important would come over their iPhones. The communiqué was stuck in with the junk ads for credit cards & magazines of coupons for fried chicken places & carpet cleaning places.

The communiqué fell in love with an ad for a carpet cleaning place. They moved into a nice though somewhat characterless duplex near the cornfields. The communiqué was interested in local politics. The ad for the carpet cleaning place was interested in chemicals & cleanliness & fibers. Somehow it worked. They got married. Great wedding. Open bar. I haven't heard from them since last year's Christmas card.

The birds still have their wings growing out of their chests. They also have their heads & a mason jar full of unsharpened No. 2 pencils growing out of their chests. Most of them have forgotten the uprising. The ones who have forgotten have their memories growing where their heads should be.

Creation Myth

In the beginning people had cornfields rather than sex parts. They had to attend to them every day or they would grow weedy & wild. People carried small leather bags filled with a variety of tweezers, chemicals & ointments with them wherever they went. They referred to them as their TC&O bags. Strangers would stop each other on the streets & compliment each other's TC&O bags. "Nice Bag," one stranger would say. "Thanks," the other stranger would respond, "I got it on sale at Macy's." "Oh, I love their sales," the first stranger would say. "Yes, me too," the second stranger would respond. There would be a moment of silence when both strangers considered saying farewell but both were oddly driven not to say farewell.

"I'm Meredith, by the way," the first stranger would say. "What a coincidence, my name is Meredith as well," the second stranger would respond. "I've seen you around the neighborhood; do you live close by?" the second stranger would continue. "Yes, I do, Meredith" the first stranger would say. And then she would say, "It's funny to call someone else Meredith." "Yes it is . . . Meredith," the second stranger would joke & both strangers would laugh slightly.

"It's not an uncommon name, but I think of it as my name alone," the second stranger would point out. "Yes," the first stranger would agree, then add "It's a family name." "Hey!" the first stranger would exclaim & place her hand across the forearm of the second stranger. "Me too!" "I have an idea," the first stranger would propose. "Let's go back to my apartment & attend to our cornfields." "Oh that would be delightful," the second stranger would say. "I'm feeling somewhat weedy & wild."

This went on for approximately ten thousand years. During that time there was no production of art or music or literature. All desires for expression & expressions of desire were channeled into the proper attendance to the cornfields. People would take polaroids of their cornfields every day & line them up on their bathroom walls to keep track of the development of the individual aesthetics of their attendance to their cornfields.

When the corn in the cornfields reached fruition, the people built new rooms on their houses & built cribs for their new ears of corn. The people bought books from Bed, Bath & Beyond that showed them how to build everything correctly. The houses were made of cornhusks. The cribs were made of cornsilk. Every night the President appeared on TV to wish every person goodnight individually. "Good night Meredith," he said. "Good night Meredith. Good night Meredith. Good night Meredith. Good night Meredith. Good night Meredith. Good night Meredith. Good night Meredith. Good night Meredith. Good night Meredith. Good night Meredith. Good night Meredith. Good night Meredith. Good night Meredith. Good night Meredith."

Creation Myth

In the beginning there was an old man with a long beard. He gathered all the children around him to sit at the foot of his chair & said to them: *I am going to tell you the story of how the world was created.*

In the beginning there was light. In the beginning there was fire. In the beginning there was the chaos of nerves. In the beginning there was the saltiness of skin. In the beginning there was the word. In the beginning there were a couple of ice cubes on a piece of sheet metal. In the beginning there were lies. In the beginning there were only lies.

In the beginning a fox fell from the sky. In the beginning the crow flew into a stone wall. In the beginning a Buick backfired. In the beginning there was silence. In the beginning there was darkness. In the beginning there was crying. In the beginning no one would talk to me. In the beginning there were starched shirts & regular distribution of medicines. In the beginning I was so lonely I chewed my fingertips off.

Just then the old man's brother walked into the room. He asked his brother: *What are you doing?*

The old man with the beard responded: *I am telling these gathered children the story of how the world was created.*

The brother looked at the room & back at the old man with the beard: *But brother, these are not children, these are mimeograph machines.*

It was at this point that the mimeograph machines began to rattle & shake. They began to discharge hundreds of copies of birth certificates onto the linoleum floor. The birth certificates formed into an enormous pile that filled the room. The pile grunted & shuffled & wheezed heavily like an injured beast.

Creation Myth

The hole I dug began to talk to me about the beginning of the world:

> There was a big glass sphere but some punk kid shot it with a BB gun & it shattered. Out of the hole sprang a university. At this university they only taught four subjects: earth, air, water & fire.

> If you got a PhD in water you had to learn the chemistry of liquids, hydraulics, the construction of swimming pools & breakers; you had to read the Icelandic sagas & Thucydides, you had to read most of Melville. You had to know the feeling of rain on your face on the beaches of Vietnam.

> To get a PhD in earth you had to study geology & new age religions, farming & mining. The more wayward members of the university taught the history of rock & roll.

> For the PhD in air one had to get one's pilot's license, one had to live on the beaches of North Carolina for a summer & work at the kite shop.

> PhDs in fire studied the effects of smoking & fevers, they studied the psychology of arsonists & the erotic allure of explosions in contemporary action films. In their final test they had to recite the combustion points of every household material.

> In order to understand anything there had to be at least four people in the room at all times. A PhD in water could only comprehend the water.

Then I told the hole this:

> *I have a PhD in holes. I know the aesthetics of stolen artwork. I interpret the meanings of lost books. I study everything that is missing. This is what I know: in the beginning there was only a hole & the hole began to speak.*

Then the hole said this:

Destruction Myth

I.

In the end there will be a bowl full of grapefruit seeds on the steps to the Lincoln Memorial.

In the end there will be a hat on the top shelf of a musty closet.

In the end there will be a suburb drowned in ocean water.

In the end there will be a child's skull filling with ash.

In the end there will be a poker hand with five fours of hearts.

In the end there will be a broken bike lock sticking out of the ice.

In the end the bears will take their bear clothes off & reveal themselves to be animals.

In the end the men will chew their own feet off.

The end will be a knotted strand of bleached-blonde hair. You will find this knotted strand of hair on your pillow & you will not be able to recall whose hair it could be.

The end will come up behind you on the left but tap you on the right shoulder so that you turn around & no one is there.

II.

Everyone saw the end coming
& threw a big party
with barbecued sausages
& moon bounces
& people swung sledge hammers wildly,
sometimes smashing a car window,
sometimes hitting an old lady
sitting in a green plastic chair,
sometimes hitting nothing more
than a low-hanging elm branch.

The ATMs drooled money
& children shredded it
& baked it into the middle of croissants.

III.

There are only three more choices available for the general public:

      1. A candle stub slowly re-erecting itself until it produces a match
      2. The embodied voice of the laser beam
      3. A porcelain toilet lacquered with honey

There will be a vote to decide which one of these three will be the end.

IV.

In the end there will be a man standing on the parched earth with a glass bowl of powdered sugar. He will toss the powdered sugar onto his sweaty body & then lie down on the parched earth to wait for the ants. But there will be no ants.

V.

It will end in taffy.
It will end in pig's blood.
It will end when the bears & the lions fight to the death.
It will end a year after the forgers are arrested.
It will rain.
There will be thunder.
There will be saltwater in the pantry.
There will be lightning in the shed.
Everyone will gnaw their hands & feet off
& then desperately try to use their remote controls.
Everyone will wear undergarments of cellophane.
Everyone will line their mouths with tiny bricks of sugar.
The cars will inherit the earth.
The power lines will inherit the earth.
The barn swallows & ducks will inherit the earth.
The unused drawing pads will be given to the thrift stores.
There will be a problem with the swimming pool.
There will be a disturbance & no one answering at 911.

VI.

The ending will be in a glass of Kool-Aid. Poisonous Kool-Aid. Either that or we'll bring back the dinosaurs through genetic tricks & they'll rampage through downtown Santa Monica. Either that or an asteroid will hit the earth. Or maybe it will just be a nuclear war. Whatever the end will be there will be delays at LAX. There will be old news in the daily newspapers, old wine in new bottles, old teddy bears in the arms of fresh children.

VII.

The ants will inherit the earth.
The Fourth of July will inherit the earth.
The monocled villains will inherit the earth.
The earth will inherit the earth.
There will be ice but no ice cream.
There will be grass but no cougars.
There will be harbors but no pirates.
There will be silk in the top drawer.
There will be dishes in the sink.

VIII.

You will go out on a date & it will last forever.
It will be an episode of *Cheers*.
It will be a river with no bottom.
It will be a bridge with no river.
They will ride in tiny brightly-colored cars.
They will hold their guns to your forehead.
It will end with an obligatory greatest hits collection.
Bottle flies ribboning out of a cow's mouth.
The actors will have no parts.
The grasses will have no seeds.
The seeds will have no salt.
The salt will have no sea.

IX.

These are the signs of the end:

They launch a viral marketing campaign.
They eat the last of the food.
They kill one another with bombs.
They kill one another with stones.
The rich give their money to the middle classes.
Music schools allow talented kids to soar.
Everyone will sell their names on eBay.
There will be fifty different choices of toothpaste.
The panthers lie down with the kindergartners.
The flies swarm & eat the pedestrians.
The oceans become blood again.

X.

Years later the history textbooks
will refer to The End
as The Intervention.

XI.

The priests are excited about the end
but the politicians consider it problematic.
The bakers continue baking their breads.
The librarians stay on the phones too long.
The ranch is overgrown with saw grass & timothy.
The sun defies the shadows.
The mice eat the snakes.
The tildes destroy the asterisks.
The bloggers post recipes for their last meals.
The Dow drops abruptly.

XII.

In the end the void will be stuffed after his third trip through the buffet line.
In the end Larry Bird will decide what he should have had for lunch.
In the end the mimeograph machines will begin to produce originals.
In the end everything that spoke a language will use a tire iron.
In the end the rubber.
In the end the coarse.
In the end the mountains.
In the end the blackberries.
In the end the Nile monitors.
In the end the stink of rotting pelts.
In the end the Formica.
In the end the nickel.
In the end the waiting.
In the end the waiting room.

XIII.

Most people didn't want it to end.
But then it was the end.

The Author

Mathias Svalina was born in Chicago, where his parents were both chemists. He is the author of five chapbooks and the coauthor of five collaboratively written chapbooks. His work has been published widely in journals such as *American Letters & Commentary, The Boston Review, Diagram, jubilat,* and *Typo.* He has won fellowships and awards from The Bread Loaf Writers' Conference, *The Iowa Review,* and New Michigan Press, among other places. With Zachary Schomburg, he co-edits *Octopus Magazine* and Octopus Books. He currently teaches writing and literature in Denver, Colorado. *Destruction Myth* is his first book.